10 PEOPLE WHO DISCOVERED AMERICA

by Bruce Black

cover illustration by Doug Byrum

text illustrations by Charles Russell

Published by Willowisp Press, Inc.
401 E. Wilson Bridge Road, Worthington, Ohio 43085

Printed in the United States of America

10 9 8 7 6 5 4 3 2 1

ISBN 0-87406-509-7

For Susan as we embark...

Contents

Introduction

Before Columbus' famous voyage in 1492, the mapmakers of the world thought there was nothing but an empty ocean between the western coast of Europe and the eastern shores of Asia. But soon after Columbus sailed to the New World, maps began to change. The world on the maps began to show the discoveries of the men you'll read about in this book.

Some of the explorers were fortune-seekers who wanted to find gold. Others were searching for a passage to the rich trading lands of Asia. Still others wanted to add to the knowledge people had of the world they lived in.

The Spanish marched and sailed north from their stronghold in Mexico to explore the southwest, while the British were settling along the Atlantic coast. The French were creating colonies around the Great Lakes and in the Mississippi Valley. The vastness of the American continent astonished these men. Its beauty captivated them, even as they exploited the lands' resources.

America wasn't discovered all at once. Hundreds and hundreds of years passed from the moment Leif Ericson first set foot on the coast of Vinland to the day that Lewis and Clark completed their two-year journey across half the continent. Each step these brave explorers took carried them farther and farther into the wilderness—toward the unknown, toward terror, even toward death. But each journey of discovery added a piece to the map that was being drawn of the New World.

The year 1992 marks the 500th anniversary of Columbus' historic voyage to the New World. This book presents the men who risked everything in the name of exploration—the men who did more than any others to discover America.

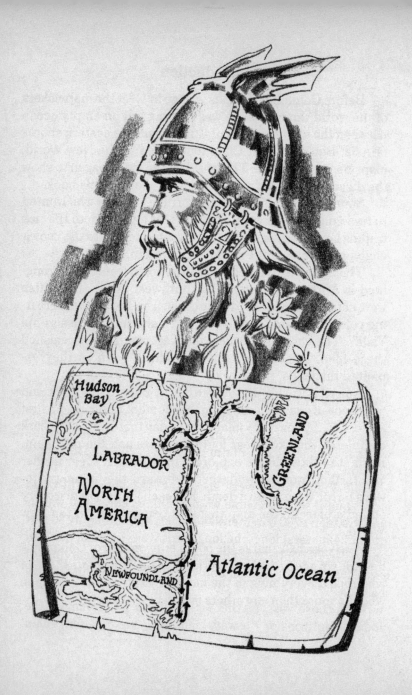

1 LEIF ERICSON
(about 970-1020)

Dragon Ships in the New World

"I beseech the immaculate Master of monks to protect my journey. May Heaven's Lord bless me and hold His hand over me."

from *The Greenlanders' Saga*

In the 11th century, Viking sailors setting out on a journey like the one in *The Greenlanders' Saga* had many reasons to pray. Ships in those days usually leaked. Without a compass, sailors had to follow the sun and the stars, relying on the weather, crude instruments, and blind luck to reach their destination.

The Viking boats were known as long ships. They had large square sails of coarse wool and lines cut out of walrus hide. Sixteen to 30 oarsmen sat on each side. Roughly 80 feet (about 24 meters) long, the long ships were made of oak and pine, with gracefully-curved sterns and bows. The carvings of fierce dragon heads on their bows helped the boats cut through the waves.

With these vessels, the Vikings from Scandinavia (the modern countries of Norway, Denmark, and Sweden) ruled the seas during the 9th to the 12th centuries. Their kingdom extended all the way to Russia and southern Italy.

A Family of Explorers

Leif Ericson's father, Eric the Red, settled on Iceland, the cold rocky island in the north Atlantic. Iceland was a viking colony. After Eric the Red was forced to leave Iceland, he sailed west for a land that he had heard others talk about. He found the island that we know as Greenland, and spent three years exploring its southwestern coast. Returning to Iceland, Eric organized an expedition of pioneers to settle the new land. They set out in a storm, steering around dangerous icebergs that drifted with the currents.

Fourteen ships arrived safely in Greenland. The settlers began to build huts along the coast. Leif, Eric's son, grew up in one of these villages on Greenland's coast. Accustomed at an early age to the harsh life of the northern climate, he was well suited to the rugged life of the sailor and the hunter. But he was also a thoughtful man.

Leif heard many stories about a flat land to the west of Greenland, a country filled with forests and game. If the stories were true, Leif thought that the timber and food might make it easier to survive the winter months in Greenland.

Around the year 1002, Leif went to visit a man named Bjarni Herjolfsson, who had accidentally sighted this new land. Once, while Bjarni was sailing from Norway to Greenland to spend the winter with his father, he missed Greenland's shore in a thick fog and sailed west into unknown waters. When the fog lifted, he saw a strange, new land, but didn't go ashore. He spent four days searching for Greenland. Finally, he and his crew spotted the familiar shoreline of home and landed safely.

Bjarni told Leif about the course that he had sailed. He

estimated how far a boat would have to travel to reach the mysterious new land. Leif was so excited that he bought Bjarni's boat and hired a crew of 35 men.

Leif wanted his father, Eric, to lead the voyage. After all, he was the most experienced explorer—he had discovered Greenland! But Eric felt that he was too old and weak to endure the hardships of a long journey into unknown seas.

A Bad Sign

Leif was as strong-willed and stubborn as his father. Finally, Eric gave in. He would lead the voyage. He mounted his horse to ride to the ship. Suddenly, the horse stumbled, throwing Eric to the ground. Eric injured his foot. He took it as a bad sign and decided to remain at home. Instead, he placed his son in command of the ship.

After getting the ship ready for the voyage, they set sail along Greenland's coast, heading north from the village. They took everything they would need until they reached land. They also took tools they would use to build homes once they arrived safely.

A New Continent

Leif steered the ship west, until he came to the southeastern shore of Baffin Island, the island that Bjarni had found. He ordered his men to cast anchor and to lower a small boat so that they could go ashore. They found no grass, no trees—only a windswept, barren coastline. It was a gray, empty land of huge glaciers and slabs of rock.

Leif was very disappointed. He called the island Helluland—the Land of Flat Stones—and returned to the ship. Leif and his crew sailed south, where they found a land covered with green forests and white beaches. Leif called it Markland—the Forest Land—and set out to sea again. Historians believe that this was Labrador, in what is now eastern Canada.

The wind carried the boat south for two more days. When they sighted land again, it was an island not far north of the mainland. Rowing a small boat ashore, they found grass covered with bright beads of dew. They knelt on the ground and licked the dew off the grass to quench their thirst.

Returning to the ship, the Vikings sailed into the narrow channel between the island and the mainland. Leif carefully steered the ship westward past the cape, despite the low tide. But the ship ran aground. The men, who were anxious to land, lowered a small boat over the side and rowed ashore.

Building the Settlement

When they reached a place where a stream flowed out of a lake, they cast anchor and explored the land near shore. Later, when the tide rose, freeing their ship, they rowed back to the ship and towed it up the river into the lake. After carrying their leather sleeping bags and equipment ashore, they started building huts as protection for the coming winter.

It was a good location. The salmon in the river were larger than any of the men had ever seen before. The grass was plentiful, so the cattle they had brought could graze freely.

After they had built their huts for the winter, Leif divided the men into two groups. One party would explore the countryside without straying too far from the base. The other group was to stay and guard the huts. Each day Leif joined a different group. One day he explored the countryside and the next he stayed near the huts.

Everything went according to plan until one night, when the group returned from their day of exploring the country, they realized that one man was missing. His name was Tyrkir, a close friend of Leif's father. He had even taken care of Leif when he was a young boy.

Leif was angry. Without wasting any time, he gathered 12 men together. But the rescue party went only a short distance from camp before they saw Tyrkir strolling toward them. He looked cheerful.

"Why are you so late?" asked Leif. "And why didn't you stay with the others?"

Tyrkir was so excited he could barely speak.

"I have found vines and grapes!" he exclaimed.

"Are you sure?" asked Leif.

"I am certain," said Tyrkir.

Because of Tyrkir's discovery, Leif formed a new plan. In the morning, he ordered his men to gather as many grapes as they could. Throughout the winter they cut vines and timber, and loaded the cargo onto the ship.

The Return Home

In the spring, they sailed away from the country that Leif named Vinland—Wine Land—in honor of Tyrkir's discovery. Many historians now believe this land was Newfoundland, although others think the Vikings got as far south as Cape Cod in Massachusetts.

With a good wind behind them, they headed east for Greenland. Soon, they saw the tall mountains and white glaciers of their homeland. But when the ship changed direction, one of the crew complained to Leif.

"Why are you steering the ship into the wind?" he demanded.

"Don't you see anything strange?" asked Leif.

The man answered that he didn't see anything unusual.

Leif pointed to a dark line on the horizon. "I can't tell whether it's a ship or a reef that I see," he said.

Finally, the others were able to make out the dark line. When they sailed closer, they saw that it was a reef. But only Leif's sharp eyes could recognize the shapes of men stranded on the reef.

"We must get close enough to help them," he said.

The ship sailed closer to the reef. When it had pulled as close as possible, they saw 15 shipwrecked men clinging to the reef. Leif took them all aboard, along with as much of their goods as his ship could hold. Together, they sailed to Greenland.

The 15 sailors gave their cargo to Leif as thanks for rescuing them. After his brave voyage to the New World and his rescue of the 15 sailors, the Viking captain became known as Leif the Lucky. He became rich and famous and was known throughout the land.

2 CHRISTOPHER COLUMBUS
(1451-1506)

Across the Sea of Darkness

ON the morning of August 3, 1492, a strong wind filled the sails of three ships—the *Nina,* the *Pinta,* and the *Santa Maria.* The ships' leader was Christopher Columbus, an Italian from Genoa. They were leaving the safe harbor of Palos, a seaport on the southern coast of Spain, to begin one of the most remarkable voyages in history.

Instead of sailing south along the coast of Africa in search of a new route to Asia, Columbus had a much more daring plan. He believed that he could reach the East Indies by sailing to the west. But to get there, he would have to sail into the uncharted waters of the Atlantic Ocean, known then as the Sea of Darkness!

It was a tremendous risk, since people in the 15th century had no way of knowing what lay beyond the sea's horizon. As far as anyone could tell, the Sea of Darkness stretched from the western edge of Europe all the way to the eastern coast of Asia—a solid mass of water unbroken by any land.

According to many calculations, the distance across

the sea was too great to cross safely. It was the fear of such a vast, unknown sea, not the belief that the world was flat, that kept ships from sailing west. Almost all educated people accepted that the world was round by the time Columbus set out from Palos in 1492. But people could not agree on the earth's size.

Some scientists relied on the calculations of the Greek astronomer, Eratosthenes, who lived in the 3rd century B.C. Others believed the calculations of Ptolemy, a man who lived more than 500 years later. Who was right?

Columbus believed that Ptolemy was right. He had maps based on Ptolemy's calculations, and a compass. With these things and his own intelligence, Columbus set sail, confident that he would discover a new route to Asia.

Destination Unknown

From Palos, he headed for the Canary Islands, 800 miles southwest of Spain, off the coast of Morocco in Africa. The islands were a good place for the ships to replenish their supplies before heading into the uncharted waters to the west.

But almost as soon as they left port, the *Pinta's* rudder broke. Martin Alonso Pinzon, the *Pinta's* captain, repaired the rudder using ropes, and the three ships continued toward the Canary Islands. But the next day, the wind and rough seas loosened the ropes holding the *Pinta's* rudder in place. Again, the crew repaired the rudder, but now the ship was leaking badly.

As soon as the ships reached the islands safely, Columbus ordered carpenters to make a new rudder and repair the leak. In the meantime, he had the ships loaded with fresh supplies for the journey: wood and water, dried meat, salted fish, fresh fruit, salt, wine, molasses, honey, and biscuits. In all, they took along enough food and supplies to last 28 days. But Columbus believed he could reach the coast of Asia in 21 days.

Trimming the Sails

Columbus also ordered the rigging on the *Nina* to be changed. He knew about the winds that blew steadily from the east throughout the year. These easterly winds would take his ships west. By changing the *Nina's* sails to square rigging, the ship would be able to take advantage of the wind.

But Columbus was one of the few sea captains who knew about the westerly winds. The westerlies were as reliable as the easterlies, except that they blew in the opposite direction. How else could he have risked sailing so far west if he had no way of returning safely?

Columbus was not only an expert seaman. As commander of the fleet, he had to know how to handle the 90 men and boys sailing with him. When the three-week delay for repairs made the crew more and more uneasy, Columbus calmed them. When the men interpreted the eruption of a fiery volcano on the island of Tenerife as an evil omen, Columbus explained away their superstitious fears.

The rudder repairs were completed on August 31. Columbus took another four days to finish loading supplies. Then, after a special service of thanksgiving, he ordered the anchors hoisted. The three ships set sail shortly before noon, taking advantage of a fresh breeze.

Into Uncharted Waters

The Canary Islands grew smaller and smaller, until they appeared as nothing more than dark specks on the horizon. On September 9, surrounded on every side by unknown waters, many of the sailors wept. Some of them were afraid that they would never see land again.

Columbus comforted his crew. He promised them that they would discover a land full of riches. But he understood that his promises could not calm his men's fears. Columbus decided to keep two different accounts of the voyage. He kept an accurate, but secret, record for himself of the distance traveled each day. And he kept another record for the crew. He was afraid they might get nervous if they knew how far the ships had sailed without reaching land.

How far could his ships sail in a day? It depended on the strength of the wind and the direction of the ocean currents. On some days, Columbus recorded sailing as many as 180 miles (290 km). But no matter how great or small the distance, he always sailed to the west.

Signs of Land?

On September 11, he saw the broken mast of a large ship floating in the sea. Two days later, the *Nina's* crew spotted two birds. This type of bird almost always stayed close to land, so the men's spirits rose, thinking that they were nearing land. But the next morning, the men saw a meteorite fall into the sea. Some of the crew members lost their courage, taking the falling meteor as a bad sign. Once again, Columbus had to calm their fears. He was able to convince them that it was a natural occurrence that didn't mean anything—just like the volcano back in the Canary Islands.

In his log book, Columbus recorded that the weather was fair with mild breezes. There were some storm clouds, and sometimes a light drizzle. So mild was the weather that Columbus claimed the mornings reminded him of the month of April in southern Spain. All that was missing, he wrote in his journal, was the song of the nightingale.

Huge patches of weeds began to appear in the water. Columbus suspected that the weeds had been torn from rocks to the west. Each day brought more signs of land— great flights of birds and thicker patches of weeds. One day the crew saw some porpoises and a white bird with a long tail. A sailor on the *Nina* killed one of the porpoises with a harpoon, and the men had a feast.

Dark Shapes on the Horizon

For the next few days, the breezes remained gentle. The sea was as smooth as a river. With the good weather, Columbus' crew was almost cheerful. The ships sailed further and further west. The *Pinta,* the fastest of the three ships, always sailed ahead to sight land. On September 18, Captain Pinzon of the *Pinta* pointed to the north, claiming to see land. Dark shapes lay 45 miles away, covered by clouds and darkness. The crew urged Columbus to change course. But Columbus, whose calculations didn't show land there, kept on course.

For 11 days the wind filled the ships' sails, carrying them further westward. But on September 19, the wind died. The three ships stood almost still, drifting slightly southwest with the current. Columbus watched small birds flying over the ship. A pelican landed on the deck. When it started to drizzle without any wind, he was convinced that he was close to land.

Whenever the wind picked up, Columbus resumed his course west. He relied on his charts and his own calculations, ignoring Pinzon's advice to look for islands to the north. Columbus wasn't interested in discovering islands.

He wanted to find a new route to Asia and he kept his course due west.

The weeds grew thicker, sometimes holding back the ships. More and more small birds began to fly out to the ships. Some of the birds were ducks.

The Terrified Crew

But despite these signs of land, the crew was frightened. The wind continued to push them west. They were worried that they would soon run out of supplies. Each day took them farther away from Spain, and many were sure they would never see their homes again. But they didn't know about the westerly winds, the winds that would blow them home again. Columbus had kept these winds a secret! He was worried that if his crew found out about the winds, they might force him to return to Europe before discovering the route to Asia.

In the next few days, Columbus saw many more birds and other signs that they were near land. Yet the men grumbled about the unpredictable wind and the flat sea, convinced that they would never see land again.

But this time, Columbus couldn't calm them. By September 24, the men were angry, muttering against Columbus day and night. They whispered and wept over their fate. They called the voyage an insane adventure. How could they have let themselves follow Columbus, a crazy man who only wanted to become rich?

Imagine how the terror-stricken crew felt. Each day took them farther into the unknown, into a part of the world where no one else had ever sailed before! How much longer could supplies last? That night they even began to talk about throwing Columbus overboard in the darkness and sailing home themselves.

But the next day, September 25, Pinzon cried out from the *Pinta,* "Land!"

Hearing the joy in Pinzon's voice, Columbus fell to his knees and thanked God. In the growing darkness, Columbus thought he saw the land, too, about 75 miles to the southwest. He changed course, planning to reach land the following day.

False Alarm

But the next morning, after sunrise, Columbus saw nothing but the endless sea, with only a handful of storm clouds hugging the horizon. Columbus decided that they must have seen clouds, which often look like land, the night before. Disappointed, he returned to his original course and continued sailing west.

It rained hard on October 1. In the gloom, Columbus reviewed his log. Since leaving the Canary Islands, he calculated that his ships had sailed 2,121 miles (3,400 km). But he couldn't tell his men. How much more terrified and angry would they be if they knew they were so far from home?

He told his ships to hold their course and watched as the boat cut across the smooth sea. There were more birds. The wind filled the sails again, and the ships made good progress the next two days.

But the impatient crew complained more and more. They felt their leader was crazy to continue. Still, Columbus did not change his course. On October 7, the *Nina* raced ahead. Suddenly, the ship's cannon rang out, and a flag was raised on her mast to show that they had found land. But there was no land. It was only another trick of the terrified sailors' minds.

The Edge of Terror

By October 9, they heard the flapping wings of birds flying above the ships all night. But on the next day, the desperate crew made Columbus agree that they would sail for just three more days. If they found no land by then, they would turn around and head for home.

Two days later, on October 11, the men saw a large flock of birds flying overhead. They spied a branch with berries on it floating near the ship. The *Pinta's* crew spotted a small board and a stick that looked like it had been carved by a person.

And then that night, after prayers, Columbus ordered that extra men be placed on the lookouts. He reminded his crew that the first man to sight land would receive a reward of 10,000 maravedies (gold coins) from the king and queen of Spain.

Later that night, around 10:00, Columbus was standing at the stern of his ship. To the west, he thought he saw a light. It looked like a candle flame flickering up and down. He called to another man, and after a few moments, he saw the light, too. But when they called a third person to confirm the report, the light vanished. *Was it land?* wondered Columbus. Or was *his* imagination starting to play tricks on him, too?

Shortly before midnight, the moon rose in the east. The decks were quiet, the men asleep. Except for the creaking of the rigging and the murmuring of the sea, the night was perfectly still.

Then, at 2:00, a cannon went off. It was fired from the deck of the *Pinta.*

Prayers Answered

The *Santa Maria* caught up to the *Pinta* as fast as it

24

could. It was then that Columbus learned that Rodrigo de Triana, one of the *Pinta's* crew, had spotted land. This time it was not a trick. The dark shapes of islands rose out of the sea to the west. It had taken more than 33 days and almost 3,200 miles (5,120 km). But Columbus had found land.

Royal Banners

In the light of the morning, the crews looked out from their ships at the islands. They saw naked men and women standing on the beach. With a handful of sailors, Columbus went ashore carrying the royal banner of King Ferdinand and Queen Isabella.

Columbus named the island *San Salvador*, Spanish for Blessed Savior. Afterward, he greeted the natives who began to gather on the beach. Their skin was brown and their hair was black. To Columbus, none of the natives looked over 30 years old.

Believing that he had arrived in India, Columbus called these people Indians, as we still do today. But he hadn't arrived in India. He had reached an island in the Bahamas, 600 miles (960 km) off the coast of North America. He was the first European to set foot in the Western Hemisphere since Leif Ericson almost 500 years earlier.

Columbus returned safely from his trip to the New World and was greeted in Spain as a hero. He made three more voyages west to seek the route to Asia. Although he discovered Central America and South America, as well as many islands, including Cuba and Haiti, he never found the route that he was searching for. On May 20, 1506, he died in Valladolid, Spain, never realizing that he had discovered a new world.

3 JOHN CABOT
(about 1450-about 1498)

The Merchant of Bristol

WE know very little about John Cabot, the first European since Leif Ericson and the Vikings to set foot on the North American continent. Columbus had reached only islands. Many historians believe that Cabot, like Christopher Columbus, was born in Genoa, Italy. His father was a merchant who moved with his family to Venice—the trading capital of the world—when John was a young boy. It may have been in Venice, or earlier in Genoa, that John learned about the spice trade.

In the 15th century, the spice trade was one of the most exciting and profitable businesses in the world. As a young man, John Cabot might have dreamed of sailing to far-off lands of the East—China, India, and Japan— and returning with ships loaded with enough spices to make him rich.

Europeans were willing to pay a lot of money for the different spices brought from Asia by ship or over land by camels. Without spices, people couldn't preserve their foods or flavor bad-tasting meat, and doctors couldn't make certain medicines.

Trade Routes to Asia

Like many others, Cabot understood that finding a shorter route to Asia would reduce the time to transport the spices. Also, traders would be able to cut costs by eliminating the middlemen along the way. These men always took a share of the profits in the spice trade.

As a merchant, Cabot believed that finding an easier, quicker route to the East could bring a man great wealth. But as a seaman, he knew the great risk and terrible danger of sailing west into uncharted and unknown seas to reach the East Indies. He may have heard stories in Venice from Icelandic merchants about a far-off land called Vinland that Leif Ericson had discovered centuries earlier. Certainly Cabot and every other merchant knew about Columbus' successful voyage. But maybe there was still another route that would lead to the fabulously-rich Spice Islands.

Cabot tried to raise money for his trip. First he went to the Spaniards, then to the Portuguese. But both countries turned him away. Columbus had already found a route for the Spaniards. And the Portuguese were more interested in sailing south around the tip of Africa. They didn't want anything to do with a risky voyage to the West.

Bound for England

That left England, the only other country that was rich and powerful enough to support such a voyage. Cabot decided to move his family to Bristol, England. Bristol was a good choice for several reasons. There was a large Italian community there, and he found the sights and sounds on the Bristol docks familiar. The docks were as crowded and lively as any in Portugal, Spain, or Italy. In the 15th century, Bristol was England's most important port on the Atlantic Ocean.

Cabot made and sold maps and charts to support himself and his family. It was a skill that he had learned as a merchant. In time, he made friends among many of the Bristol merchants. Cabot discussed his plans for a voyage to Asia with these men. They were interested in his idea and were willing to back him with money if he could gain permission from the king. If Cabot was successful in finding a route to Asia, they thought, Bristol would become the richest port in all of Europe.

The merchants of Bristol were very eager to discover some way to increase their sagging business. The trade of wool and salt to Iceland for fish had fallen off. Many merchants were hoping to find new places to fish and new markets in which to sell their wool.

Legendary Islands

And if Cabot sailed west, they thought, perhaps he might discover the Island of Brasil and the Island of the Seven Cities. Bristol sailors had been searching for these imaginary islands for years. They were supposed to have fabulous treasures. Of course, no Bristol sailor had ever discovered them. But as they sailed the seas in search of them, they found new routes west in the process. Sometimes they even caught glimpses of land to the south and west of Greenland!

Cabot persuaded the merchants that he could discover a new route to the Spice Islands by sailing west. He'd bring the spices back to Bristol, making the merchants of Bristol the richest in all of Europe. It wasn't long before they were willing to invest in the voyage and help Cabot get to London for a meeting with the king.

King Henry VII listened closely to John Cabot,

because he had earlier turned down Columbus' request for support. The king wanted his country to discover new lands and sources of wealth. King Henry knew that if Cabot could find a route to Asia, it would give England a monopoly on the spice trade. And since the Bristol merchants were providing the money for the trip, that meant that he didn't have to pay for it with England's money. King Henry was willing to lend his support to the voyage.

A Royal Charter

On March 5, 1496, King Henry granted John Cabot a charter that gave him permission to explore new lands. But at the same time, it limited the areas where he could explore. The king didn't want Spain and Portugal to think that he was trying to steal away some of the lands that they were exploring.

With royal permission to search for new lands to the west, north, or east of England, Cabot began his voyage. But he was forced to return to England because of bad weather and problems with his ship.

After more preparations, Cabot and 20 men set out around May 22, 1497. After leaving Bristol, Cabot steered for Dursey Head on the southern coast of Ireland. From there he headed southwest into the Atlantic, searching for the legendary Island of Brasil and the Island of the Seven Cities.

An east-northeast wind blew strongly, and Cabot sailed west for 32 or 33 days. On June 21 or 22, his ship ran into a severe storm. On June 24, he sighted land. According to his calculations, he had reached the North American continent somewhere between Cape Canso, Nova Scotia and Cape Breton on Cape Breton Island.

With the help of his men, he carried ashore a wooden cross and banners in honor of the Pope and Henry VII. After claiming the land for England and Christianity, Cabot explored the shore within sight of his ship.

On the beach he found a stick of red wood, about 18 inches long, pierced at both ends. A little further away, he found an old campsite where someone had made a fire. There were snares, a netting needle, and cuts on trees. All these things meant that people lived nearby. But Cabot wouldn't let his men stray too far from the ship. He was afraid that the natives might be unfriendly.

Along the Coast

Historians are not sure what happened next. Cabot might have continued sailing south or he might have turned north again. He claims to have sailed 300 leagues (about 900 miles or 1,440 km) along the coast before returning to England.

The return trip took only 17 days. When the ship landed at Bristol, the merchants and everyone else welcomed Cabot back as a hero! As a reward for his discoveries, King Henry gave him 10 pounds in cash and a pension of 20 pounds a year.

Then, in May of 1498, Cabot set out again with five ships, hoping to return to what he thought was Asia. He never returned and no trace of his ships was ever found. But John Cabot remained a very important figure in history. The English based their claim on North America on Cabot's discoveries. Thanks to him, the English were able to spread their empire over almost the whole continent. And that's why almost 300 million people in Canada and the United States speak English today!

4 GIOVANNI DA VERRAZZANO
(about 1485-1528)

Exploring the Atlantic Coast

NOT until 1523 did France join England, Spain, and Portugal in exploring new routes across the ocean to Asia. The voyage was begun because France's king, Francois I, needed money to help pay for a war with Spain. At the time the king didn't know that Giovanni da Verrazzano, an Italian navigator, had a plan that might solve his money problems.

Verrazzano had heard about the excellent fishing off the Newfoundland coast. And he knew about the supply of gold in the New World. One of his ships had captured three Spanish galleons loaded with gold and silver treasures from Mexico.

In addition, Verrazzano had heard about Magellan's successful return to Spain with spices from the East. But Magellan's trip, although a success, was difficult because of the long, dangerous voyage around the southern tip of the New World.

The Northern Shore

But what about the northern shore of the New World?

It was unexplored. Perhaps an explorer could discover a shorter route to Asia by sailing north around the continent.

This was the plan that Verrazzano proposed to the French king. Many merchants, his friends and business associates, supported his plan. He convinced the king that such a plan—if successful—could lead to enormous wealth for France. Francois I decided to send Verrazzano across the ocean. He was hoping Verrazzano would find a new route to Asia for France. He also hoped that he would explore the possibility of trade in the New World.

Verrazzano was a master navigator. He purchased the most up-to-date navigational equipment for the voyage. Before sailing, he had his ship, the *Dauphine,* outfitted with heavy cannons. And he arranged to store enough supplies on board to feed a crew of 50 men for eight months.

On Board the *Dauphine*

The *Dauphine* sailed from an island in the Portuguese Madeiras on January 17, 1524. Verrazzano set a course that was due west. They encountered a treacherous storm during the long voyage before sighting land off the North Carolina coast on March 7. From the *Dauphine* that day, Verrazzano looked out on a landscape that clung low to the horizon. Great fires illuminated the sky. Seeing the fires, Verrazzano was convinced that the land was inhabited.

Sailing south along the coast, he looked for a good place to anchor. But then he became afraid of meeting the Spanish if he continued too far south, and turned north again. When he finally cast anchor, he sent a small boat to the beach.

Many Indians stood on the sand watching the boat make its way through the surf. The Indians wore grass skirts or animal furs. In a letter, Verrazzano wrote that they wore garlands made from the feathers of birds. Their skin was dark. Their hair was black and thick, but not very long. Sometimes, he noted, they tied it in the back of their heads in a little tail.

As for the shore, tall sand dunes ran along the beach for miles. Large and small rivers emptied into the sea. New buds and blossoms in the forests and fields, bursting forth in spring, astonished him. The trees and flowers gave off a pleasant aroma that Verrazzano and his men smelled a hundred leagues away.

Verrazzano sailed north along the present-day North Carolina coast. He went past the eastern shore of what is now Virginia and Maryland. At one point he sent a young sailor swimming ashore carrying bells and mirrors as gifts for the Indians. As he explored the coast, he gave names to the bays and islands. He was the first European explorer to name sites in the New World after prominent people and places in the Old World.

Indians

Continuing north, he noted many deer, rabbits, and birds. Somehow, he missed the wide entrance to Chesapeake Bay. Anchoring near the bay, he sent a handful of men ashore to explore the land. The men came back and told him about a land of many lakes, rich with wildlife. They found an old woman and a young girl with a group of children. The crew took one of the children on board the ship and then back to France with them.

Further north there were fewer flowering trees. But there were wonderful flowers—wild roses, violets, and

35

lilies—and many wild herbs. The Indians, Verrazzano noted, used different tools to hunt birds and animals. They used traps or snares. Their bows were made of hard wood, and their arrows were formed from reeds, with bones for arrowheads. To fish, they used dugout canoes to paddle into the sea.

The beauty of this land reminded Verrazzano of the part of Greece called Arcadia. He named the region Arcadia for its peace and beauty. Exploring further north along the coast, Verrazzano anchored between two small hills—now called Staten Island and Brooklyn—which today serve as the entrance to New York's harbor. This passage of water is known today as the Verrazzano Narrows.

The friendly natives welcomed him warmly. Their clothes were made of the feathers of colorful birds. Some of the natives pointed out a safe place for him to land the small boats that he used to explore the shore.

If not for a sudden storm, which forced Verrazzano to leave the bay, he might have spent more time exploring the Hudson River. But he had no choice. He couldn't risk having his ship thrown against the shore and wrecked.

From New York harbor he sailed east, reaching a triangular-shaped island—Block Island—off the coast of what is now Rhode Island. But bad weather forced him to sail northwest along the coast until he reached Narragansett Bay. Verrazzano named the bay Refugio.

He anchored off the coast, not far from where the city of Newport stands today, and discovered more Indians. These natives were even friendlier than those he had met farther south. For 15 days, Verrazzano stayed in the shelter of the quiet bay, making friends with the Indians and learning about them and the new land.

How the Natives Lived

During his stay, he was invited to inspect the natives' dwellings. Verrazzano described the mats of straw that protected the Indians' huts from rain and wind. Some of the dwellings, he reported, held families of up to 30 people.

On May 6, with the skies clear, Verrazzano ordered his ship to leave the sheltered bay. Continuing further north along the coast, he navigated the ship through the dangerous currents off Cape Cod. Then he came to what is now called Casco Bay, Maine.

Dressed in bearskins, the natives at this place were hostile to the strangers. They wanted only knives, hooks for fishing, and sharp metal tools instead of trinkets. When 25 men of Verrazzano's crew tried to explore the land, the Indians attacked them. It's not surprising that Verrazzano called this region the Land of the Bad People.

Return to France

By the beginning of June, he grew concerned about the shortage of supplies on the ship. He had left France in January with eight months of supplies. Now, seven months later, he decided to end the voyage and return home.

He had reached as far north as Cape Breton before turning his ship east. The *Dauphine* sailed into Dieppe harbor in France on July 8, 1524. Verrazzano had failed to find a sea passage to Asia. But he had explored a continent larger than his own Europe.

5

HERNANDO DE SOTO
(about 1500-1542)

The Child of the Sun

HERNANDO de Soto was one of many Spaniards to sail across the Atlantic in search of riches. He was not the first Spaniard to set foot on Florida's shore. But de Soto probably explored the New World more thoroughly than anyone else in his era.

Born around 1500 in Spain, de Soto sought his fortune with nothing but a sword and shield as soon as he was old enough to enlist in the army. He was a brave soldier and was sent to Peru around 1531, where he became known for his courage and skill in battle against the Inca Indians. He gained a fortune of more than 100,000 gold pesos. Upon his return to Spain, the king rewarded him for his service. He made de Soto governor of Cuba. But he also gave him the right to explore Florida and what is now the southern part of the United States, keeping any riches that he might find.

With his wife, Dona Ysabel, de Soto set sail in April, 1538, with five ships. They landed in Santiago, Cuba. The ships were sent on to Havana, where de Soto gathered supplies and trained his men. Then, in May, 1539, de

Soto sailed from Havana with nine ships, leaving his wife to rule the island. On May 30, he landed near Tampa Bay on the west coast of Florida, the long, narrow peninsula that Spain considered the entrance to the continent.

Quest for Gold

From the beginning, his search for gold was a ruthless, relentless quest into the rugged wilderness. He constantly drove his 620 men in their heavy metal armor. In addition to the hundreds of soldiers, de Soto took with him 223 horses and a food supply of 13 live hogs, which increased to several hundred along the journey. The expedition also included four priests, four friars, four women, and many workmen for building bridges and boats and repairing equipment like armor, boots, and shields.

It took several days to unload the equipment and supplies off the boats onto the beach. While the ships were unloading, de Soto sent out a scouting party of men on horses. They met a handful of Indians and killed two.

Soon afterward, de Soto captured an abandoned Indian village near the landing site. After looting the buildings, de Soto and his men destroyed the huts and the temple.

In June, needing guides and slaves to carry the expedition's baggage, de Soto sent out a party to capture Indians. But during an attack on a band of Indians, one of the men claimed to be a Spaniard. Sure enough, his name was Juan Ortiz. He had survived an earlier Spanish expedition to Florida and had lived with the Indians for 12 years. His ability to interpret the Indians' language for de Soto was a great help to the expedition. And without him as a guide, de Soto's band might never have found its way through the wilderness.

Cruelty

Pushing his men northward from Tampa Bay, de Soto followed the coastline along the western edge of the peninsula. He marched with his men past lakes, through swamps, and alongside fields of corn. Along the way, the Spaniards burned villages and captured natives. They treated the Indians with great cruelty, sometimes throwing the Indians to specially-trained dogs who tore their flesh off.

As the Spaniards followed the main Indian trails inland, they came to other villages. They took prisoners, looted huts, took supplies and food, and burned the villages. In most villages, de Soto kidnapped the chief, then fought off the Indians who tried to save him. Easily defeating the Indians, who did not have modern weapons, the Spaniards took more than 300 slaves. The Indians were forced to march in chains through the wilderness, carrying the supplies of the Spanish explorers.

In an abandoned Indian village called Apalache further north, de Soto and his men set up camp for the winter on October 6. The Indians had run from their homes to escape the invading army. They left behind stores of food and fields ready for harvesting.

A Hard Winter

For five months the men rested, waiting out the winter. There were almost 500 Spaniards and an equal number of prisoners. The Indians hated the Spaniards who had made them slaves. That winter many of the Indians had to live without clothes or shelter. Chained together so they could not move, a good number didn't survive the winter.

One Indian managed to slip past the guards and set fire to the town. A strong wind fanned the flames. Before the Spaniards could put out the blaze, nearly two-thirds of the town was destroyed. As punishment, de Soto ordered the Indian's hands cut off. According to a priest who witnessed the punishment, the Indian showed no fear or pain.

In March, 1540, the men began moving again. De Soto ordered the men to carry with them as much corn as possible. But which direction should they follow to find gold? De Soto had heard a story from a captured Indian about his homeland in the Northeast, where much gold was buried. De Soto set off to find the village, marching his men into what is now southern Georgia.

Heavy rains swelled the swamps and rivers, making travel slow and difficult. The men waded through thick mud. They passed through a valley, where they captured 700 more Indians to serve as slaves. Indians who refused to lead the Spaniards further were killed. One was burned alive.

Treasure at Last

Finally, on April 30, after two months of travel, they arrived at a small town on the Savannah River, just below present-day Augusta. They found no gold, though, only freshwater pearls. De Soto filled a chest with pearls for himself. The Spaniards, raiding tombs and homes, took whatever they wanted. In addition to the pearls, they stole the Indians' corn and kidnapped their queen.

It had been one year since de Soto had left Havana. But he still had not found any gold. Hearing about yet another land of gold, he marched his men north, crossing the Blue Ridge Mountains in search of treasure. During the passage through the mountains, the Indian queen, along with three other slaves, escaped. But de Soto, who had no further use for her, let her go and continued on his journey.

At villages along the way, the Indians gave the Spaniards roast dog meat and corn. They also had no choice but to give the Spaniards fresh slaves. On June 3, the men came down the Tennessee River and crossed the Appalachian Mountains. It was the first time these mountains were ever crossed by Europeans.

In Search of Cosa

The men rested for two weeks, until the end of June, on an island just above what is now the Alabama state line. Then de Soto started south again. He took the chief of the village as hostage and followed the Tennessee River southwest in search of Cosa, a chief who knew about buried treasure. The first thing de Soto and his men did when they reached Cosa's village was to take the chief prisoner, along with men and women from his village. The Indians looked on helplessly as the Spaniards looted their village. With Cosa as his prisoner, de Soto left the village and went south on August 20. He met little resistance in village after village. But still he found no gold.

After releasing Chief Cosa, de Soto continued further south into the land of the Mabila. A great chief—tall and with a mantle of feathers that reached his feet—met them. He, too, was taken prisoner. He had to supply over 400 men and 100 women as slaves for the Spaniards.

The Deadly Dance

But when de Soto and his men entered the village of

the Mabila, the Indians greeted them with a dance that suddenly turned into a surprise attack! They fought all day, burning the town, along with most of the Spanish baggage, including de Soto's chest of pearls. More than 3,000 Indians died in the battle. Only 22 Spaniards were killed.

While his injured men recovered, de Soto ordered the rest of his men to camp in the town. After repairing their equipment, they destroyed the surrounding countryside. De Soto refused to give up his dream of finding gold and went north on November 14. Then, turning west, he headed toward the Mississippi River and camped for the winter in two Chickasaw Indian towns. On Christmas Day, the Spaniards huddled around fires, barely sheltered from a heavy snowstorm.

That spring, the Indians attacked one day at dawn. Surprised, the Spaniards were forced to retreat from the burning buildings. They lost a dozen men, more than 50 horses, 300 pigs, and much of their equipment. They moved to another village not far away and built a new forge to repair their weapons and armor. Ten days later, when the Indians attacked again, the Spaniards were ready and beat back the attack.

Turning Westward

The Spaniards then turned westward, exploring parts of the Lower Mississippi Valley. They reached the broad river on May 8. Always, de Soto kept searching for gold. And always, he failed to find it.

During the winter months, de Soto ordered his men to build a stockade around their camp at Utiangue. They remained there for four months. Heavy snows forced the Spaniards to stay in their huts for a month. With the warmer spring weather, de Soto and his men broke camp and headed south along the Quachita River.

After more than three years, de Soto had not found a single nugget of gold or silver. And the one chest of freshwater pearls had been lost in an Indian raid.

A Terrible Loss

After the explorers started out, they suffered a crucial loss. Juan Ortiz, their guide and interpreter, died. Without him, the Spaniards had to find their own way.

Then de Soto became sick with a fever. After three years of wandering in hopeless search of treasure, Hernando de Soto died on May 21, 1542. His body was wrapped in cloth and loaded into a canoe. At night, his men paddled out into the middle of the river and secretly threw his body, weighted with sand, into the Mississippi River. They were afraid the Indians might attack them if they found out that de Soto, the great fighter, was dead.

Dressed only in rags, 311 of de Soto's men managed to reach Mexico safely a year later. More than four years of searching through the southern part of the continent yielded them no gold or silver. But de Soto will always be remembered as the first European to explore the great Mississippi River.

6 FRANCISCO VASQUEZ DE CORONADO
(about 1510-1554)

The Seven Cities of Gold

WHILE de Soto was exploring the southeastern section of the continent, another Spaniard was searching for gold in the deserts of the southwest. His name was Francisco Vasquez de Coronado.

Born into a noble family, Coronado came to Mexico in 1535 with the Viceroy Mendoza. Coronado was the governor of New Galicia, the most northern section of New Spain, as Mexico was called then. In February, 1540, he too got the disease that so many of his countrymen had in the New World—gold fever! He decided to organize an expedition.

Coronado sent out two men to scout the region of New Galicia. A Negro slave named Esteban, a survivor of an earlier expedition, served as guide to Fray Marcos de Niza. They went north together with a handful of Indians. When they reached Sonora in northern Mexico, Fray Marcos sent Esteban ahead with a few Indians. He told him to send back a cross as a sign if he had made any discoveries. A larger cross meant a greater discovery.

True or False?

Each day another Indian messenger returned to Fray Marcos with a larger cross. The Indians told him that the Seven Cities of Gold lay just ahead. Covered with jewels and glittering in the bright sunlight, a magnificent city spread out across the desert, with houses four stories high. Even greater cities, they said, lay beyond.

Making his way through Arizona's mountains, Fray Marcos sent a messenger to tell Esteban to wait for him at the edge of the wilderness. But Esteban ignored the message. Alone, he approached the pueblo huts of the Zuni Indians. He always showed his medicine man's rattle—a dried gourd. For the Indians he had met in the south, this had been a sign of peace. But to the Zunis, the rattle was a symbol used by their enemies!

Esteban was imprisoned in a hut on the outskirts of the village. He managed to escape. But the Indians chased after him and caught and killed him. After he heard the bad news, Fray Marcos climbed a nearby hill and looked into the distance. From the top of the hillside he could make out the tall pueblo huts of the Indians. He returned to Mexico and reported his findings. The Seven Cities, he said, were built of stone, not of gold or silver.

Coronado in Command

But the Spanish in Mexico refused to believe Fray Marcos. They still believed in the myth of the Seven Cities of Gold. They organized a huge expedition and placed Coronado in command. The force included more than 300 Spaniards and 800 Indians, many horses, sheep and pigs, perhaps 1,000 servants and workmen, and many friars to convert the Indians to Christianity. They set out on February 23, 1540. Two ships also sailed up the coast of southern California to carry supplies and search for a water route to the Seven Cities of Gold.

Coronado led his force up the western coast of Mexico. In April, with about 50 horsemen and foot soldiers and most of the Indians, Coronado left the slowly moving main force at Culiacan. He hoped to reach the Seven Cities more quickly.

Along the way they met natives who gave them the small fruits from cacti. There was little else they could offer, since it was the end of the dry season. Most of the supplies from the previous year's harvest were gone.

Coronado and his men reached a temple that was a landmark on the road to the village of Cibola. They were near the edge of the southeastern Arizona grassland. Beyond rose the hills and mountains of the high country.

Supplies Run Low

Following rivers and streams, Coronado marched northeast. It wasn't long before the men had used up most of their supplies. Three Spaniards died from eating a plant, not realizing it was poisonous. But the Indians, used to living off the land, did not go hungry. They reached a river with reddish water and continued through the southwestern section of Arizona. This river is known today as the Little Colorado—the Spanish word for *red*. They traveled eastward until they reached Cibola.

After a brief struggle, Coronado captured the village. But he was very disappointed. There was no gold in the village. It didn't even look like the villages in Mexico, as Fray Marcos had told them. Coronado cursed the small, cramped, poor village, with its stone and clay huts. But the Spaniards ransacked houses and stole food and anything else that they thought was valuable.

The Grand Canyon

Coronado sent a messenger to the main force's commander, Melchior Diaz. He ordered Diaz to bring the rest of the troops to Cibola. As soon as Diaz arrived, Coronado sent him with a few troops to explore the region beyond the Colorado River to the west. Coronado also sent another smaller force northwest of Cibola. There they found the Grand Canyon. But the huge canyon blocked their path and they couldn't get around it. They had to turn back.

With the main army, Coronado marched into the middle of New Mexico and set up winter quarters in Tiguex, a small village on the River Grande. The Indians there were peaceful. They were farmers, not warriors.

There was plenty of corn, beans, squash, and turkeys to eat. But it was a cold winter, and the Spaniards weren't prepared for the harsh weather. Instead of building their own shelters, they forced the Indians out of their homes. Like de Soto, Coronado and his men looted the village and raided storehouses of food, until finally the Indians attacked the Spanish force.

The Spaniards fought off the Indians and took many prisoners. Coronado tortured his prisoners with more cruelty than even de Soto had used.

Following the Turk

Coronado still wanted only one thing. In the spring, he left Tiguex in search of legendary towns of gold. He went across the plains, marching as far as the Oklahoma border. Leaving the main force behind him, Coronado went ahead with about 30 horsemen. They rode northeast for almost six weeks.

Leading Coronado's small band was an Indian guide

named the Turk. The Turk told fantastic stories about a land where fish were as large as horses and gold was everywhere. He promised to lead the Spaniards to this fabulous land.

But Coronado didn't know that the Indians had bribed the Turk to lead the Spaniards away from their villages. The Turk led Coronado on and on, across the flat plains. They ate buffalo meat until they were sick of it. The Indian tribes they met were not afraid of the invaders.

When Coronado's band reached the center of what is now Kansas, he finally decided that he had seen enough herds of buffalo and poor Indian tribes. "We have wandered long enough," he told his men. They had discovered no gold, no silver—nothing but dirt-poor Indian villages and buffalo bones.

Then the band turned on their guide. Using an iron collar that strangles a victim—they tortured the Turk to his death. Coronado and his men returned to Tiguex on the River Grande for the winter. If there was no gold, at least Coronado and his men had plenty of food there.

Journey's End

Coronado had spent two years searching for gold. He had lost his own fortune. Finally, he decided he had had enough—he was ready to return to Mexico. In April, 1542, Coronado led his men back home.

Even though he never found the fabled Seven Cities of Gold, Francisco Vasquez de Coronado had learned more about the southwestern United States than any other explorer. Before his journey, no one could have imagined the land's incredible vastness. He had helped to show how large the New World really was.

NEW FRANCE
(CANADA)

James Bay

NEWFOUNDLAND

Saguenay River

St. Lawrence River

Ottawa River

Lake Champlain

Port Royal

Great Lakes

Atlantic Ocean

7 SAMUEL DE CHAMPLAIN
(about 1570-1635)

Father of New France

WHEN Samuel de Champlain made his first voyage
to Canada at the age of 36, he had already sailed
at least six times across the South Atlantic. He had
learned much about Spanish America from the islands of
the West Indies, including Puerto Rico and Cuba, and
Mexico.

Champlain was not the first explorer to carry the
French flag to Canada. The Italian navigator Giovanni
da Verrazzano, sailing for France, had first seen Canada
in 1524. And Jacques Cartier was the first to explore the
coast off Newfoundland and the St. Lawrence River for
France. Although Cartier never found the Northwest
Passage to China, he made three voyages to Canada. Each
time he returned to Europe with exciting reports of the
furs, fish, and other natural resources of the land across
the sea.

But it was the young Champlain who opened up
Canada's western frontier. He sailed in March, 1603,
almost 60 years after Cartier's explorations. His drawing
skills and map-making ability came in handy.

It was not an easy voyage for the crew. Halfway across the Atlantic the fleet of ships ran into strong gales and dangerous icebergs. Wicked winds blew steadily for 17 days. By the time the ships reached the Grand Banks off the coast of Newfoundland, it was May 2.

Up the St. Lawrence

A thick fog blanketed the Gulf of St. Lawrence, and Champlain's ship passed through Cabot Strait in the fog. He couldn't see a thing. All he could hear were the tremendous waves breaking against the treacherous rocky coast. When the fog finally lifted, he could make out the coast. But another gale tossed the fleet out to sea again.

Finally, on May 27, the ships anchored in the St. Lawrence River at Tadoussac, the center of the French fur trade. On shore, the Indians had prepared a great feast. Champlain and his men saw great kettles of stew made from moose, beaver, and bear meat and seal blubber. After smoking the pipes that the Indians passed around, the explorers ate the stew—and they liked it! But they didn't like the way the Indians cleaned the grease off their hands. They wiped them on their own hair or on the backs of their hunting dogs!

On June 11, Champlain spent the day exploring the area around the village. A week later, Champlain headed up the St. Lawrence in a longboat with Indians as his guides. At a bend in the river, Champlain saw a place of rich forests and beautiful meadows that he called "Kebec." He later founded the great city of Quebec there.

He continued up the river until he was stopped by some of the rapids. Later, these same rapids got the name *La Chine* (French for China), because the explorers thought they led to China. But Champlain's rowboats were too heavy to go any further. Without lighter canoes made of bark, Champlain had to turn back. Before leaving, he learned from his guides about the enormous lakes above La Chine and about the great falls of the Niagara River.

Furs and Dried Fish

In mid-August, the ships were loaded with furs and dried fish and the explorers returned to France. Champlain published a record of his voyage, describing in great detail the land, its resources, and the Indians.

In March, 1604, Champlain returned to Canada. He explored much of the unknown coastline to the south of the Gulf of St. Lawrence. Many of the maps that he drew of the small harbors and coves are still considered accurate by sailors today, even though they are more than 300 years old.

Soon Champlain was given his first command by the French king. He was asked to explore the western and northern coastline of Acadia for a site where the French could build a temporary settlement. In a small boat, Champlain and 11 men sailed up and down the coast.

Champlain decided to build a settlement on a small island in the middle of a river. The flagship then returned to the site to build shelters, using glass and wood that they had brought over from France. The work was very hard, partly because mosquitoes and black flies kept attacking the men.

Building a Village

When the village, named Sainte-Croix, was finished, it contained a storehouse, barracks for the men, a forge, two blocks of houses for the officers, and a small chapel. There was also an outdoor oven for baking bread and a handmill for grinding grain. Each man also had a small garden plot.

Before winter, Champlain set out twice more to explore the coast. First, he headed up the Bay of Fundy again to investigate reports that there was copper there. On his voyage he met friendly Indians wearing beaver skins. But he returned without finding any copper.

Then, on September 2, he sailed southwest in a boat fitted with sails and oars to explore the coast of New England or, as it was known then, Norumbega. He was searching for a place to build a permanent French settlement.

Staying close to the coast with his crew of 12 Frenchmen and two Indian guides, he saw the southeastern coast of Maine through breaks in the fog. He passed near Mount Desert Island. Heading further south, Champlain reached Penoboscot Bay.

Champlain continued south, reaching as far as the Kennebec River in Maine, when foul weather and short supplies made him decide to turn back. It was October 2 when he returned to Sainte-Croix.

Winter of Death

Less than a week after his return, heavy snow fell. Harsh winds blew against the French settlement. Within two months, three or four feet of snow lay on the ground, and the river was blocked by ice. With the rest of the 79 men, Champlain endured the biting cold, and reduced rations without complaint.

Only half the men were still alive by the time the warmer weather arrived in March. Without fresh vegetables to supply vitamin C, most of the men died of scurvy, a painful disease that inflames gums and causes swelling of the arms and legs.

In June, Champlain decided to look for a better location for a settlement. While sailing as far south as Cape Cod, including a tour of Boston Harbor and the Charles River, he made navigational charts of the coast. Along almost the entire route, the French were welcomed by the Indians on shore. Most of the Indians were farmers, with well-tended fields of corn, beans, tobacco, and squash.

But Champlain wasn't sure he could trust the Indians. So he turned north on July 25 and returned to Sainte-Croix in August. He found a spot further north, which he called Port Royal. It was on the opposite side of the Bay of Fundy. And it was protected from the cruel northern winter winds by the hills of Nova Scotia.

A New Settlement

Using timber and supplies from Sainte-Croix, the men built a new village before the onset of winter. The new huts gave the men confidence that they could survive. But even though it was a mild winter, with rain falling as often as snow, men became ill. The rainwater seeped under the cabins, making the floors damp. Twelve more men died of scurvy, despite a kind Indian chief who provided them with food.

Champlain spent much of the dreary winter revising his maps. And he planned new voyages, too, hoping to discover the route to China with the coming of spring.

In early March, winter ended. Champlain began another journey to New England. But bad storms forced the ship to return to Port Royal with a broken rudder. It wasn't until September that he was ready to sail again. This time he returned to Cape Cod, reaching as far south as Nantucket Sound. He sighted an island, perhaps Martha's Vineyard, but turned back after a number of Frenchmen were wounded in an ambush by some unfriendly Indians on shore.

By the time he reached the coast of Maine, the ice was already two inches (five cm) thick. And it was only November. There were still another five months of winter. But luckily for the French, the winter of 1606-1607 was a mild one at Port Royal. Still, the men struggled against scurvy, with four more dying.

A Wooden Cross

In the spring, Champlain returned to the Upper Bay of Fundy, searching once more for the copper without any luck. Instead, he found a moss-covered wooden cross at one spot on the shore. It was the sign of a previous, unknown expedition. On September 3, 1607, after the wheat was harvested, Champlain and his men sailed for France.

It was the last time that Champlain would see Acadia. But it was not his last visit to Canada. Less than one year later, having passed his 40th birthday, he returned to Quebec. Champlain realized that the French needed to be closer to the fur trade. This would let them buy fur pelts from the Indians more cheaply. And with a strong port on the river, the French could control the waterway into the wilderness.

Landing at Quebec on July 3, Champlain established his settlement on the bend of the St. Lawrence River. This would be his home, except for trips to France, for the rest of his life. Men cleared the woodland, dug ditches, and planted winter wheat, rye, and grapevines in preparation for the winter. Flies and mosquitoes swarmed around them.

Indians or Skeletons?

Once again it was a harsh winter. Half the French fell to scurvy. Even the Indians suffered in the bitter cold. Champlain offered what little food he could to the Indians. He wrote that many of them looked like skeletons. They ate their dogs and gnawed at their leather moccasins and robes. Only Champlain and eight other Frenchmen of the original 24 survived the winter.

To secure French settlements along the river, Champlain realized that he needed to form an alliance with the local tribes. In the spring, Champlain joined the Hurons, the Algonkins, and the Montagnais on the warpath against the Iroquois. With 60 warriors, he traveled down the broad river of the Iroquois. The river emptied into a great lake that Champlain named after himself—Lake Champlain.

At the start of the battle, Champlain fired his musket at three opposing chiefs. His shots killed two and wounded the third, frightening off the rest of the Iroquois, who fled into the woods. In celebration, the Hurons, the Algonkins, and the Montagnais danced and sang, feasting for three hours. Instead of joining the Indians, Champlain went to explore Lake George.

A Mighty River

Champlain learned about a great river that the Indians claimed extended all the way to Florida. He wished that he had more time to explore this great river. One month later, Henry Hudson, the Dutch explorer, was to sail up that same river in search of a passage to China. It now bears his name.

In May 1613, Champlain followed the Ottawa River with four other Frenchmen and an interpreter. Their plan was to explore the region that he had heard so much about. After carrying the canoes, known as *portaging*, past the rapids at La Chine, they paddled upstream, through endless woods and fields.

The deeper Champlain traveled into the wilderness, the more surprised were the Indians who greeted him. The Indian chiefs who saw Champlain joked that he must have fallen from the clouds. It was rare for a white man to travel across such difficult territory. Sometimes the men had to carry their canoes and supplies overland to reach the next lake or stream. And of course, they had to fight the mosquitoes and flies the whole way.

Still, Champlain pushed on toward Hudson Bay. But the journey proved to be too far. Champlain realized that his French interpreter and guide had been lying about the route to the north sea just to earn a reward. Instead of going further, Champlain turned back. He had reached Lower Allumette Lake.

But the flame of discovery still burned in Champlain. After a brief visit to France, he headed north again in 1613. In canoes with two other Frenchmen and 10 Indians, Champlain followed the Ottawa River past Lower Allumette Lake into the Mattawa River, 75 miles (120 km) further north.

Lake Huron

The party continued upstream, reaching Lake Nipissing in what is now Ontario province, on July 26. Champlain thought the lake, with islands and fish and meadows along its shore, was beautiful. From Nipissing, Champlain took the French river north into the majestic Lake Huron, the fifth largest lake in the world.

He had first heard about the great lake in 1603, more

than 10 years earlier. But he had never believed that he would see it in his lifetime. Along the way he collected information about other lakes, expanding French knowledge of the wilderness. From his explorations, he began to understand how vast the continent truly was. It was much larger than anyone had first thought.

At 45, Champlain's days of exploration were not over. He spent the rest of his life helping France's new settlements in the new land. He died on Christmas Day in 1635.

8 RENE-ROBERT CAVELIER, SIEUR DE LA SALLE
(1643-1687)

Master of the Mississippi

IT was during one of Canada's long, hard winters that Rene-Robert Cavelier, Sieur de La Salle, a fur trader living near Montreal, first heard about the river called the Mississippi. Two Seneca Indians who had come to trade furs for food and knives told him of the great rivers—the Ohio, which they called *Beautiful Water,* and the Mississippi, which they called *Big Water.*

The dream to explore the Big Water took hold of La Salle. But it took months of planning before he could begin his journey in search of the passage through the North American continent. He was in desperate need of money. And he also needed permission from the governor of New France, as Canada was known then. Finally, after the winter snow melted and the days had grown longer, La Salle set out.

In Search of the Big Water

He had hired 14 men, four canoes, and several Indians as guides, with two of their own canoes. They were joined by a group of Catholic missionaries in three canoes who hoped to convert Indians they met along the way. The nine canoes entered the St. Lawrence River below the La Chine rapids on July 6, 1669, and headed for Lake Ontario. Although he did not know it, La Salle would not return to Montreal until late fall of the following year.

Journeying into the wilderness began to take its toll on the men after only the first month. Loaded with supplies, the canoes were difficult to maneuver down the river. It was back-breaking labor to carry the canoes overland whenever the river became too shallow or where rapids made the river too dangerous to pass. Sometimes these portages through dense forest and swamps lasted for miles. La Salle pushed the men hard, breaking camp at dawn and traveling until dusk. He knew the long summer days wouldn't last forever.

By August they had reached Lake Ontario, where they met a tribe of Seneca Indians. Leaving some of his men to guard the canoes, La Salle went with the Indians back to their camp. He hoped to convince them to guide him to the Ohio River.

Captured!

But the Indians had other plans. They held La Salle and his men captive for four weeks because they wanted to discourage them from exploring any further into their territory. It wasn't until La Salle told the Indians that he had changed his plans that they released him.

And he *had* changed his plans. From a friendly Iroquois he met while being held captive, he learned that

64

he could reach the Ohio more easily by heading south from Lake Erie. With the Iroquois Indian as his guide, La Salle rejoined the men guarding his canoes.

When they crossed the Niagara River, with the roar of the great falls in the distance, it was already the middle of September. Although the days were still warm, the nights were growing cooler. La Salle knew he had only another month, two at most, before the rivers would freeze and make travel impossible. How far could he get before then?

The Copper Trail

The group reached the Iroquois' home. The Iroquois gave La Salle a Shawnee captive, Nika, as a guide. Nika knew the route to the Ohio River. While La Salle was at the Iroquois' home, two other Frenchmen emerged from the woods. Like La Salle, they had been pushing through the wilderness. But rather than looking for a passage to China, they were searching for copper along the shore of Lake Superior. One of the men was named Louis Joliet.

When the missionaries heard Joliet's descriptions of the Indians in the region, they decided to leave La Salle and journey toward Lake Superior. Then some other of La Salle's men left the expedition to return to Montreal. La Salle, meanwhile, headed south along Lake Ontario with Nika in search of the river that was the entrance to the Ohio.

With Nika's experience, La Salle made his way to the Ohio River. But as the days grew shorter and the nights colder, his men began to grow afraid of continuing the journey. Cold rains fell, soaking the men to the skin. And then came the snow, reminding the men of the severe winters of Canada. The group reached the falls of the

Ohio—the site of Louisville, Kentucky, today—and made camp. The men cursed the weather and the lack of food. They thought it was insane to try to continue. That night, while La Salle slept, the men sneaked away. They wanted to return to Montreal before the heavy snows trapped them in the wilderness without food or shelter.

Alone!

When La Salle awoke, he found only Nika beside the fire. He realized that it would be impossible to continue the voyage. He returned to Montreal in the late fall of 1670 with his canoe loaded with furs to sell. But his dream of finding a passage to China was all but shattered.

One thing La Salle realized was that the rivers were too narrow in some places and too shallow in others. Even if one of the rivers did lead to the Pacific, no ship larger than a canoe would be able to make the passage.

But La Salle understood that even if the rivers didn't lead to the Pacific, they were very important for another reason. They were the easiest way to transport the valuable furs from the interior of the continent to the ports. From the ports they could be shipped to Europe, where they would bring high prices.

Controlling the Rivers

Slowly, La Salle began to understand that if the French controlled the rivers, they would also control the land—and the fur trade! Ever since the French had arrived in North America, they had traded food and tools to the Indians in return for furs. It was the key to French power and wealth in the New World.

By the time La Salle returned to Montreal, he had another plan to propose to the governor. This time La

Salle would find a route leading to the Mississippi—the river that Indians said stretched from the Great Lakes to the Gulf of Mexico! Discovering and controlling this river would not only give France a much bigger area for its fur trade. It would also give France command of more territory in North America than either England or Spain could claim.

Through the Great Lakes

In August, 1671, La Salle and Nika set off in canoes with a handful of French woodsmen. They made their way down the St. Lawrence to Lake Ontario, past Niagara Falls and into Lake Erie. Then they went up the Detroit River and entered Lake Huron, following its western shore through the Straits of Mackinac into Lake Michigan.

At the southern end of Lake Michigan, Nika pointed out the entrance to the Chicago River, a narrow stretch of water no larger than a European canal. They steered the canoes into the river and followed it until they had to carry the canoes overland to the Des Plaines River, which flowed into the Illinois River. When they reached another river that joined the Illinois, Nika told La Salle that they had reached the Mississippi.

Down the Mississippi

La Salle floated south down the winding Mississippi, reaching the northern border of what is now Tennessee, before turning back. He was afraid to meet the Spaniards, who controlled the southern portion of the river. But he knew his mission was only half completed. He had discovered the great route to the center of the vast continent. Now he had to convince France to defend it.

A new governor named Frontenac was in command of New France (the name the French gave to their territory in Canada) when La Salle returned to Quebec. La Salle quickly convinced him to build forts on the shore of Lake Ontario. La Salle felt they were needed to control the trade between the Indians and the English and Dutch. These two countries had been cutting into French profits.

It took three years to build Fort Frontenac at the north end of Lake Ontario. But when it was completed, it provided France with a base that was nearly 200 miles (320 km) further inland than Montreal, the closest French city. The French would be able to control the fur trade in ways that were impossible from Montreal.

After Fort Frontenac was completed, La Salle got permission from King Louis XIV to build more forts. With the help of Henry de Tonty, an Italian, and Father Louis Hennepin, a Franciscan friar, La Salle built a new fort at Niagara Falls. It would control the gateway to the Great Lakes and the fur trade that lay to the west.

The severe winter made it difficult to build the fort. But as soon as the shelters were finished, the men began work on a ship to patrol the lake and transport furs from one end to the other. They christened the ship in the spring of 1679.

The *Griffon*

The Indians who saw the ship, called the *Griffon* (a legendary animal, half-eagle, half-lion), thought it was a floating fortress as it sailed across Lake Erie toward the Straits of Detroit. By September, the boat had set its course for Lake Michigan. At Green Bay, La Salle rejoined his advance party of fur traders, who had trapped a large number of animals. La Salle loaded the furs on the *Griffon* and ordered the ship to return with its cargo to Fort Niagara. Tonty, in the meantime, was scouting the land for more furs.

While the *Griffon* was making its way east, La Salle took four canoes and 14 men and headed south along Lake Michigan. But soon they ran short of food. They had planned to meet Tonty on the Saint Joseph River, but he failed to arrive on time. La Salle's men were fearful of being trapped by the harsh winter and encouraged him to move on. But La Salle waited for his friend. When he finally came, they set off together with the men down the Saint Joseph.

La Salle's plan was to spend the winter among the Indians. He planned to build a small fort to serve as a base for the following spring. Then workers could begin building a ship to explore further south along the Mississippi.

But very little went right that winter. The Indians he met tried to talk him out of going further down the river. Hearing fantastic tales of monsters and rapids and evil spirits, some of his men deserted camp. One of La Salle's men even tried to poison La Salle's food!

Fort Heartbreak

He began building Fort Crevecoeur (French for heartbreak) on a hill on the south bank of the Illinois River, near present-day Peoria. Fort Crevecoeur would include a blacksmith shop, barracks, a shack for storing ammunition and supplies, and a small chapel.

After he saw that work was started, La Salle set out for Fort Frontenac, a distance of more than 1,000 miles (1,600 km), to gather supplies. When he returned to Fort

Crevecoeur in the fall of 1681, he found a terrible disappointment. Indians had burned Fort Crevecoeur. There was no sign of any of his men—only the burned ruins of the fort.

Still, La Salle would not be frightened away from his plan to explore and control the Mississippi River. In February of 1682, he started down the river with a small band of men. By April, La Salle and his men had paddled far enough south on the river to smell the sea. Finally, on April 9, La Salle entered the Gulf of Mexico.

Into the Gulf

Paddling to shore near the Mississippi's mouth, La Salle set a cross in the ground. To the cheers of his men, he claimed the entire Mississippi Valley for France. He called it Louisiana after his king, Louis XIV. The next day they headed north again.

Later, in France, La Salle was given a hero's reception. The country was thrilled by his adventures. He made several more trips to the New World, but his final one ended in tragedy.

In 1685, La Salle set up another fort near what is now the city of Corpus Christi, Texas. Within two years, the fort was desperately in need of help and supplies. La Salle decided to take a few men with him and travel overland to the Mississippi River. He would travel up the river to Canada to get help for the village.

Murder!

But he spent months searching for the river without finding it and his men grew more and more impatient and angry. One night, after a fierce debate over the little food they had left, one of the men shot La Salle in the head. They left his body in the bushes.

Some of the men went to live with the Indians. Others made their way to Quebec and then back to France. They spread news of La Salle's discoveries, and his name joined the ranks of the world's greatest explorers.

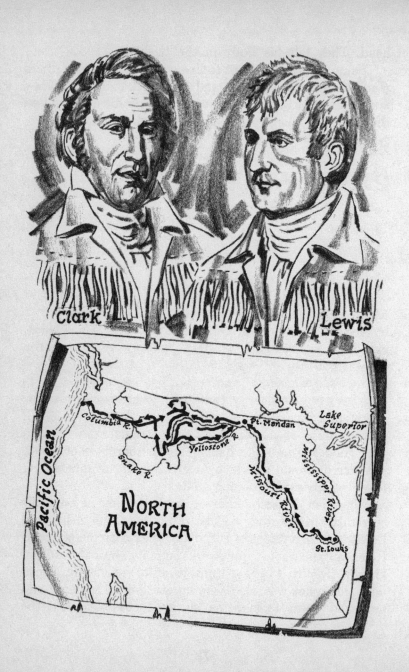

9 MERIWETHER LEWIS
(1774-1809)
WILLIAM CLARK
(1770-1838)
By Order of the President

THOMAS Jefferson, the third President of the United States, was a very curious man. Jefferson wanted to experience and understand everything. And soon after he became President in 1801, he decided to send explorers into the immense western wilderness beyond the Mississippi River.

In 1803, when Jefferson proposed the exploration to Congress, no one knew if there was a waterway across the continent connecting the Atlantic and Pacific Oceans. If such a route existed, it would save valuable time shipping goods around the dangerous southern tip of South America. It would also give America great advantage over other countries in the fur trade.

The man Jefferson chose to lead this journey was his secretary, Meriwether Lewis. The president instructed Lewis to form a Corps of Discovery to explore the Missouri River. Lewis was to follow the mighty, but almost unknown, river to where it emptied into the Pacific. President Jefferson was also very interested in Indians, and he asked Lewis to learn as much as possible about the

Indians who lived in the western territory. And, because Jefferson was an amateur scientist, Lewis was to keep detailed notes on the soil, land, animals, climate, and minerals he found during his journey.

A Secret Mission

But in the beginning, the mission had to be kept secret. The territory he would cross belonged to foreign nations. All of the Louisiana territory belonged to France. Beyond Louisiana lay land along the Pacific coast claimed by Spain, Britain, and, further north, Russia.

Congress approved $2,500 to pay for the expedition and Lewis began gathering his supplies and men for the trip in March, 1803. Each man in his company had special skills. Some men were carpenters or blacksmiths, others were hunters or boat builders. There were a handful of Frenchmen, all experienced in wilderness travel. And there was even a dog, Lewis' large Newfoundland dog, that would accompany the party the whole way.

To get ready for the trip, Lewis studied medicine and science, ordered boats and guns and ammunition, and had even prepared a special dehydrated "portable soup" in case they needed emergency rations. Along with everything else, he took a collapsible, lightweight iron frame for a canoe that he designed himself. It weighed only 44 pounds (20 kg), and he called it, "The Experiment."

A Partner

The group would travel in a flat-bottomed keelboat, a shallow, covered riverboat usually used to haul freight, and some small rowboats. While Lewis was waiting in Pittsburgh for the boat to be finished, he got a letter from William Clark, the man he had invited to share command of the expedition. A former army commander and an expert woodsman, Clark was anxious to join his friend. Clark would bring along his personal servant, a black man named York. They agreed to meet at the Falls of the Ohio River—modern-day Louisville, Kentucky— where Clark lived with his older brother, George Rogers Clark, a famous Revolutionary War general and a great frontiersman.

The Louisiana Territory

But President Jefferson had a great surprise up his sleeve. On March 9, 1804, when Lewis and Clark were getting ready to start on their journey, Jefferson bought the entire Lousiana Territory from France. The new land Lewis and Clark would explore was now part of the young United States! It was the deal of the century! The U.S. paid about 15 million dollars for more than 820,000 square miles (2,123,800 square km) of land. That's about five cents a square mile!

Setting Off

Clark and about 40 men started out from the small camp north of St. Louis in May, 1804, to begin the journey up the Missouri River. Two days later the group of explorers landed at St. Charles, the oldest white settlement on the river. There they took on two more Frenchmen to help navigate the boats up the river. Lewis joined them on May 20, and the next day the group headed into the wilderness.

Along the way they met traders and Indians who gave them information about the land they were exploring. Sometimes they covered as many as 20 miles (32 km) a day, sometimes as few as five miles (seven km). The men camped along the sandy banks of the river or on islands, or they slept in the boats.

Hunters went out each morning to bring back fresh meat. There were enough animals—bears, deer, rabbits, squirrels, ducks, geese, and wild turkeys—to keep the expedition well supplied. The men also caught fish and gathered berries.

While the keelboat made its way up the river, with Clark at the helm, Lewis walked along the riverbank, drawing different plants and animals in his sketchbook. He knew that President Jefferson wanted detailed reports on everything they saw.

Moving the boats upstream was hard work. Sometimes strong winds threatened to throw the boats onto the river banks. When the storms left, bugs came out. Mosquitoes, gnats, ticks, and flies covered the men as they struggled up the river. In July, the heat gave some of the men sunstroke. If there wasn't enough wind to fill the boat's sail, the men had to row. If the water became too shallow, they had to wade into the river and use towlines to pull the boat.

Following the River

By June 26, they reached the Kansas River, where Kansas City is located today, and rested for four days. After traveling nearly 400 miles (640 km) due west, they next followed the river north. Less than a month later, they reached the Platte River, where they met their first Indians. Lewis wanted to tell the Indian chiefs that the Louisiana Territory was now owned by the United States and he also wanted to make friends with the Indians to ensure the expedition's safety.

On August 2, six Indian chiefs appeared at the campsite and accepted gifts from Lewis and Clark. They listened to the Americans' speeches about friendship and peace and displayed with pride the medals that Lewis had given them.

The Land of the Sioux

These Indians had been friendly. But the party was about to enter the territory of the dreaded Sioux, the most warlike Indians on the journey. Passing through present-day Nebraska and Iowa into South Dakota, the men noticed the change in the landscape. There were fewer trees, and prairie grass covered the land. Herds of elk and buffalo grazed on the grass. And the men also saw prairie dogs, antelope, mule deer, foxes, and coyotes.

On September 23, two Indian boys swam across the river to the camp. They told the explorers that a band of Sioux Indians were camped at the next river. Lewis and Clark gave the boys tobacco to take back to their chiefs. They asked that the chiefs meet with them the next day.

The men waited anxiously for the meeting. The Sioux controlled trade on the river by bullying and plundering goods. If the expedition was to succeed, Lewis and Clark knew that they would have to stand up to the Sioux.

Even though some of the Indians tried to make trouble for the explorers, Lewis and Clark would not be bullied. When 200 Sioux warriors appeared on the river bank with guns and bows and arrows, the Yankees raised their rifles. The Sioux then left without trouble, and news of the explorers' bravery and strength spread throughout the area.

Black Paint?

Other Indians they met, like the Arikaras in South Dakota, were friendlier. Almost all of the Indians were astonished by the sight of York, Clark's black servant. The Indians had never seen a man with black skin before. And thinking that the color was paint, they tried to rub it off!

As the nights grew colder, Lewis and Clark began looking for a place to camp for the winter. They found a site near the friendly Mandan Indian villages. It was almost 1,600 miles (2,560 km) and five months from their starting point.

Sacagawea

During the winter, Lewis and Clark hired more interpreters to help make meetings with the Indians easier. One of the interpreters was a French Canadian trapper named Charbonneau. This man asked if he could bring along his pregnant, 17-year-old Shoshoni Indian wife. Her name was Sacagawea.

At the beginning of April, the ice began to break up and the river flowed freely again. Lewis sent the keelboat down the Missouri to St. Louis with trunks filled with notebooks, cages of live animals, and boxes of rocks and bones and plants for President Jefferson. Then, using six small canoes and two rowboats, Lewis and Clark started north. With them went Sacagawea and her newborn baby boy.

They reached the mouth of the Yellowstone River on April 25. On April 29, Lewis and one of the men killed a grizzly that weighed 300 pounds (135 kg). A few days later, they saw their first moose.

A Fateful Choice

They traveled through more rugged country, until, on May 26, they spotted the snow-capped peaks of the Rocky Mountains in the distance. Here, Lewis and Clark were faced with a decision. The Missouri River forked into two branches. If they chose the correct branch, they would reach the Shoshoni Indians, Sacagawea's people, in time to buy horses and cross the mountains to the Columbia River. But if they chose the wrong branch, they would lose valuable time. A mistake that would make it impossible to cross the Rockies before winter.

They chose the south fork. They were hoping to come to the great waterfall that the Indians had told them about—the sign that they had made the right choice. On June 12, Lewis heard the thunderous roar of the falls! He knew that if they reached the Shoshoni in time, the party could make it through the Rockies.

The men built wagons to carry the boats and supplies past the waterfalls. It was 18 miles (29 km) over some of the most difficult territory they had yet seen. The men's feet were sore and swollen. Their skin was torn from the sharp rocks. The sun blazed down on them all day, except when sudden storms sent large hailstones down on them. And at night they barely slept, afraid grizzlies would attack. But by July 4, the party had made it past the falls. The portage had taken a whole month.

In Search of the Shoshoni

Now they knew time was running out for them to find the Shoshoni. They couldn't cross the Rockies without horses. But it wasn't until over a month later that the expedition met an Indian woman and two young girls. Lewis handed them gifts, and they led him to their tribe. They had found the Shoshoni. The chief, Chief Cameahwait, turned out to be Sacagawea's brother!

They had crossed the Continental Divide. The rivers now ran west to the Pacific rather than east to the Atlantic. After a two-week rest, the men started off again. They were riding horses bought from the Shoshoni to the country of the Nez Perce, the Indians of the "Pierced Noses." Their guide was an old Indian named Toby.

The trail was steep and rocky, and sometimes it was covered by snow and ice. Many of the horses lost their footing and slipped backward. Toby led them to a trail that wound into the Bitterroot Mountains. The men were exhausted and worried. Ahead lay the most difficult part of their journey.

The Lolo Trail

The Lolo Trail clung to the sides of cliffs and mountains 6,000 feet (1,800 meters) high. On September 12, the men started out on the narrow path. Before too long, the horses lost their strength and gave out, unable to climb any farther. The men struggled for breath in the thin air. Heavy snow fell and the path was blocked. Yet they pressed on, their eyes half-blinded, their hands and feet almost frozen. Food supplies were so low that they had to eat the "portable" soup that Lewis had brought. They even slaughtered a colt for food.

But finally, on September 19, after passing the highest point on the trail, their ordeal was almost over. Ahead the men spotted a wide plain. Two days later they met up with the Nez Perce Indians, who offered them dried salmon, berries, and roots. Lewis and Clark started building canoes to continue the journey.

To the Pacific

By October 16, they reached the broad Columbia River, which Clark noted was very clear and filled with salmon. And the Indians were friendly. They stood on the banks and called out greetings to the explorers. Lewis and Clark noticed that the Indians wore jackets usually worn by British or American sailors. They knew they couldn't be far from the sea, where the huge trading ships anchored.

By November 7, they had passed through the Cascade Mountains. There they endured thick fog, rough water, and heavy winds. It rained for 11 days in a row. But a week later, they reached the Pacific Ocean. They saw tall waves pounding against the rocks and looked back on their miraculous journey. They had walked, rode, or paddled over 3,000 miles (4,800 km), the first Americans to safely cross the continent. The information they took back to President Jefferson would prove invaluable in helping the country settle the vast new territory.

10

JEDEDIAH STRONG SMITH
(1799-1831)

The Greatest of the Mountain Men

IN 1822, a St. Louis fur company placed this ad in the local newspaper:

TO ENTERPRISING YOUNG MEN

The subscriber wishes to engage 100 young men to ascend the Missouri River to its source, there to be employed for one, two, or three years. For particulars, inquire of Major Andrew Henry near the lead mines in the county of Washington, who will ascend with, and command, the party; or of the subscriber near St. Louis.

Wm. H. Ashley

In the 1820s, St. Louis was the starting point for many fur traders. These brave men, also known as mountain men, journeyed up the Missouri River into the wilderness beyond the Rocky Mountains toward the California coast. Many of these men joined fur trading companies like the Missouri Fur Company or the American Fur Company, spending months or years in the wilderness. They lived like the Indians who came to trade with them. Some went into the wilderness and were never seen again.

83

A Hardy Easterner

The advertisement ran in the newspaper for more than a month. It attracted the eye of one 24-year-old man from the east who had come west hoping to explore the wilderness in the footsteps of his heroes, Lewis and Clark. His name was Jedediah Strong Smith. In the 10 years that he crisscrossed the wilderness as a trapper, he would become one of the most important explorers in American history.

Unlike most mountain men, who couldn't read or write, Smith had received a good education. He arrived in St. Louis with his favorite books in his pack—the Bible and the *History of the Expedition of Lewis and Clark.* Men who met Smith reported that he rarely went anywhere without his rifle or his Bible. And he bathed and shaved every day, living as close to a civilized life as he could in the wilderness.

When the tall, confident Smith answered the ad and joined the Ashley-Henry expedition, he found himself among some of the men whose names would become legends in the west—Jim Bridger, Hugh Glass, Etienne Provost, Mike Fink, and others. Despite his proper eastern upbringing and education, Smith felt comfortable among these men of the wilderness. He learned from them much that his school education had not taught him.

Face to Face with Terror

Smith showed his bravery on the first expedition when he helped fight off a band of Arikara Indians. In less than a year, he had mastered the art of wilderness survival. Ashley was impressed with the young Easterner's courage. He needed men like Smith to lead trapping expeditions and to find new areas where beavers were still plentiful. By 1823, Smith was leading a party into the mountains. Suddenly, without any warning, he came face to face with one of the most frightening dangers of the wilderness—a grizzly bear.

It was late in the afternoon. The group was passing through a valley. The men were walking single file through some heavy brush at the bottom of a valley. From out of nowhere, a grizzly attacked the center of the line. Then the bear ran toward the head of the line and attacked Smith.

In a few horrible seconds, the attack was over. Smith lay bleeding on the ground. The bear had torn open his scalp and bitten off his ear. No one in the party except Smith had any medical training. Writhing in pain, he had to instruct one of the men how to sew up his head with needle and thread. As soon as the man finished, Smith mounted a horse and rode a mile to a good camping spot. After 10 days of rest, he returned to the trail. For the rest of his life, he bore the scars of the terrible few moments of the grizzly's fury!

The Trappers' Fair

The group moved on. They journeyed through South Pass, one of the routes that pioneers would use to travel through the Rocky Mountains. Stopping to trap beavers as they explored the unknown territory, the men loaded the pelts onto their horses. They returned in the spring of 1825 to a rendezvous point on one of the forks of Green River. In this area, a kind of fair was held, where trappers met to trade their pelts, buy supplies, drink, and gamble away their profits. From this rendezvous, Ashley returned to St. Louis with enough furs so that he could get out of the fur trade. He sold his shares of the company to Jedediah Smith, David Jackson, and William Sublette.

The Country of Starvation

As one of the owners of the fur company, it was Smith's job to find new regions to trap beaver. He knew the beaver population was rapidly declining in the northwest. So, in August, 1826, Smith took 15 men to explore the region near the Great Salt Lake in what is now Utah. They followed the Virgin River south out of the mountains onto a barren plain, a land so dry and desolate that Smith called it a Country of Starvation. Here, no plants grew and no animals were seen. If Smith was going to find new regions for trapping beaver, he would have to look somewhere else.

Without water or food, the party struggled west for days. They had to kill their horses for food. Finally, they reached the home of the Mojave Indians and rested for two weeks. The Indians treated them well. The trappers replenished their supplies, traded for horses, and regained their strength.

When they started out again, two Indian guides led the men over an ancient Indian trail through the desert. The trip took 15 days through the blazing Mojave Desert. Half-starved and blinded by the dust and the heat, the men reached California in November.

Meeting the Governor

Camping near the Franciscan mission of San Gabriel, Smith left his men and went to San Diego to see the Spanish governor of California. Since he was no longer on American soil, he needed permission to enter the territory to trap. But the governor suspected Smith and his men of spying for the U.S. He ordered them to leave the country by the route they had come.

But Smith ignored the governor's order. The lure of better trapping lands was stronger than his fear of the governor's soldiers. He headed north, hoping to find beaver streams in the lush northern mountains and valleys. And after traveling 300 miles (480 km), he found northern California a paradise, with plenty of beavers and other game to trap.

After spending the winter in the San Joaquin and Sacramento Valleys, Smith tried to return to the Bear River rendezvous by crossing through the Sierras. On his first attempt, after losing five horses to the bitter cold and deep snow, he turned back. From his camp on the Stanislaus River near what is now Yosemite National Park, he tried again, taking only two men with him this time.

Bitter Cold and Deadly Heat

Despite the bitter winds and very deep snow, Smith and the two men crossed through the mighty Sierra Mountains in eight days. The men survived, but three of the horses died from the cold and snow. Next they faced the cruel Nevada desert.

To escape the blazing sun and to preserve the moisture in their bodies, they buried themselves in the sand during the day and walked at night. When their food supply ran out, they ate one of their horses. On June 27, after one man had died, Smith and the remaining man spotted the sparkling surface of the Great Salt Lake. One week later, their arrival at the Bear River rendezvous was greeted with a salute from a small cannon. It was the first time that anyone had crossed the Sierras and the unknown desert country—and lived to tell about it!

Ten days later, Smith was heading west again, this time with 15 men and two women. He planned to return to the camp that he had left in northern California and to explore more of the southwest. Traveling over nearly the same route his first expedition took, he arrived again at the home of the Mojave Indians. He hoped to replenish supplies and to rest before making the trek across the desert.

Indian Attack

But as Smith and eight men were crossing a river on rafts, the Indians suddenly attacked the rest of the people waiting on the bank. They killed the men and held the two women prisoners. Smith and the men ran toward a cluster of trees as hundreds of Indians pursued them. They had only five rifles. The rest of the men made spears by tying butcher knives to the ends of branches.

Hopeless Odds

When one of the men asked Smith if he thought they had a chance, Smith said yes to lift the man's spirits. But Smith knew that the odds were hopeless. He really believed the Indians would slaughter all of them. The Indians inched toward the men using the bank of the river and rocks for cover. Smith ordered two of his men to shoot. They killed two Indians and wounded a third.

The Indians retreated to better cover, and as soon as it was dark, Smith and his men escaped, heading west on foot into the desert. Again, Smith endured the heat of the desert. But this time he made the journey in an incredibly short nine days. The only water he and his men could get was from chewing pieces of cacti.

The Accused Spy

On September 18, 1827, Smith finally returned to northern California. He found his original group at the camp on the Stanislaus River. While he was gone, they had trapped a large number of beavers and now had huge stacks of pelts. Smith left camp after a few days to meet with the Spanish government representative at San Jose. He was thrown in prison as a spy. He had entered the country illegally, and the Spanish were afraid that he was trying to claim the territory for the U.S. But once again, Smith convinced the governor that he would leave California.

However, it was impossible to find a clear passage through the Sierras in January. Smith couldn't leave California until spring arrived. Instead, he led his men north, following the coast. They reached Fort Vancouver, in spite of cold weather, low food supplies, and grizzly bear and Indian attacks. Smith and his men spent the winter at Fort Vancouver.

After several more years of trapping and exploring, Smith sold his shares in the company in 1830 and returned to St. Louis. He wanted to return to civilization, where he could enjoy his wealth.

Return of the Mountain Man

But the mountain man could not stay long in the fine city. By the spring of 1831 he had agreed to lead a wagon train of settlers to Santa Fe in New Mexico.

With 85 people, including two of Smith's brothers and 23 wagons, Smith took the expedition out of St. Louis on April 10, 1831. They were headed toward the Cimarron River, in what is now Oklahoma. To reach the Cimarron, they took a route through a region as dry and barren as any desert Smith had yet crossed. But after three days without water, the group failed to reach the Cimarron. Horses started to collapse.

Jedediah Smith knew that the groups desperately needed his survival skills—it was a matter of life and death. He went out in search of water. He disappeared over a small hill and was never seen again.

Death of a Legend

When the wagons arrived safely in Santa Fe, one of Smith's brothers saw an Indian carrying Jedediah's rifle and pistols. He demanded to know how the man had acquired them. The Indian explained that he had traded with the Commanche Indians for them. The Indians had claimed that 15 or 20 of their braves had killed Smith at a waterhole.

Legends grew up around the greatest of all mountain men. His brave exploits opened the eyes of many Americans to the vast resources in the west. His maps and journals helped pioneers reach the land that lay beyond the Rocky Mountains.

But no one will ever know the great explorer's fate.

Here are some books you can find at your library that will help you learn more about the great explorers in this book.

America's Western Frontiers by John A. Hawgood. Knopf, New York, 1967.

The American Heritage History of the Great West by David Lavender. American Heritage Publishing, New York, 1965.

The Beaver Men by Mari Sandoz. Hastings House, New York, 1964.

Champlain: The Life of Fortitude by Morris Bishop. Knopf, New York, 1948.

Christopher Columbus by Gianni Granzotto. Doubleday, Garden City, NY, 1985.

Columbus by Bjorn Landstrom. Macmillan, New York, 1966.

The Discoverers, edited by Helen Delpar. McGraw-Hill, New York, 1980.

The Discovery of North America by W.P. Cumming, R.A. Skelton, and D.B. Quinn. American Heritage Press, New York, 1971.

England and the Discovery of America: 1481-1620 by David Beers Quinn. Knopf, New York, 1974.

The European Discovery of America: The Northern Voyages by Samuel Eliot Morison. Oxford, New York, 1971.

The European Discovery of America: The Southern Voyages by Samuel Eliot Morison. Oxford University Press, New York, 1974.

The Incredible Journey of Lewis and Clark by Rhoda Blumberg. Lothrop, Lee & Shepard, New York, 1987.

Jedediah Strong Smith: Fur Trader from Ohio by D.W. Garber. University of the Pacific, Stockton, CA, 1973.

John and Sebastian Cabot by Henry Kurtz. Franklin Watts, New York, 1973.

Journal of First Voyage to America by Christopher Columbus. Albert and Charles Boni, New York, 1924.

The Journals of Lewis and Clark, edited by Bernard DeVoto. Houghton Mifflin, Boston, 1953.

La Salle: The Life and Times of an Explorer by John Upton Terrell. Weybright and Talley, New York, 1968.

Lewis and Clark: The Great Adventure by Donald Chidsey. Crown, New York, 1970.

Lewis and Clark by Roy Appleman. U.S. Department of the Interior, U.S. National Park Service, Washington, D.C., 1975.

The Lewis and Clark Trail by Calvin Tomkins. Harper and Row, New York, 1965.

Life and Voyages of Christopher Columbus, part one by Washington Irving. Cooperative Publication Society, New York, no date, reprint of 1893 edition.

The Log of Christopher Columbus, translated by Robert H. Fuson. International Marine Publishing Co., Camden, Maine, 1987.

Meriwether Lewis: A Biography by Richard Dillon. Coward-McCann, New York, 1965.

The Norse Atlantic Saga by Gwyn Jones. Oxford, New York, 1964.

The Old West: Trailblazers by Bill Gilbert. Time-Life Books, New York, 1973.

The Pathfinders by Gerald Rawling. Macmillan, New York, 1964.

Robert Cavelier de La Salle by W.J. Jacobs. Franklin Watts, New York, 1975.

Samuel de Champlain: Father of New France by Samuel Eliot Morison. Atlantic-Little Brown, Boston, 1972.

Sixteenth Century North America: The Land and the People as Seen by the Europeans by Carl Ortwin Sauer. University of California Press, Berkeley, CA, 1971.

Spain in America 1450-1580 by Edward Gaylord Bourne. Barnes & Noble, New York, 1962.

This Reckless Breed of Men: The Trappers and Fur Traders of the Southwest by Robert Glass Cleland. Knopf, New York, 1950.

The Westerners by Dee Brown. Holt, Rinehart, and Winston, New York, 1974.

Westward to Vinland by Helge Marcus Ingstad. St. Martin's, New York, 1969.

About the Author

BRUCE BLACK has always enjoyed studying history. He grew up in New Jersey, a haven for spies during the Revolutionary War. He used to travel to lower Manhattan, where he could look out at the same hills Verrazzano saw when his ship sailed into New York's harbor on his voyage north along the Atlantic coast.

Now Bruce lives in Ohio, where he works for a newspaper and writes children's books. He lives near the farm where Jedediah Strong Smith spent part of his boyhood before heading west to become one of America's bravest explorers.